FROM HURTING TO HEALING

The Offensive Playbook on Healing From Trauma

CORDARIUS WILLIAMS, M.Ed.

Published in West Palm Beach, Florida, by Cassy's Touch Publishing, LLC. www.cassystouch.com

The publisher is not responsible for websites (or their content) not owned by the publisher.

Visit the author's website at **coachwilliamsu**.com

ISBN: 979-8-9892358-3-4 (softcover)

Library of Congress Control Number 2025904953

Printed in the United States of America

Dedication

This book is dedicated to my beautiful wife, Lashundra.
Thank you for always being there for me.
Without you, this book would not be possible. I love you.

Table of Contents

Foreword

I have the honor, pleasure, and privilege to write this foreword for this transformative book that was written by an individual who is intimately familiar with the healing process.

I met Cordarius as a client who was ready to become an author but not completely clear on where and how to start. I immediately knew that he had everything he needed inside of him to write a book. My task would be to get *him* to see that.

Each session, I watched him go through the healing process on a deeper level. It would've been easy for him to tap out or procrastinate to avoid unresolved issues, but Cordarius dug deep because he knew that his healing process had a deeper purpose. He knew that his healing carried his legacy. He knew that you would pick up this book, read it, and get the answers and clarity that you have been praying for.

Cordarius practically and powerfully laid out the healing process making each layer digestible and sustainable. I encourage you to take your time to read. Embrace each word and each phrase. Allow it to sink in deep and soothe your wound. You are on the brink of receiving the answers to your next level – healing and wholeness.

From Hurting to Healing…

The content on these pages contain the answers that you've been silently praying for. What are you waiting for? Flip the page and begin your new journey *From Hurting to Healing.*

Tiffany White
Author, Writing Coach, Speaker
Simply Tiffany

Introduction

My name is Cordarius Williams, and I want to welcome you to the beginning of the rest of your life.

For the better part of a decade, I taught middle school Math. I chose to teach math because it has many problems that students need help solving.

Throughout the years, I have noticed how students become discouraged because they already know they aren't good at math. This bothers me because they give up before they even try.

Another thing that I noticed during my time as a teacher is that these students are not only dealing with unanswerable Math problems but also have unanswerable life problems.

They struggle with depression, anxiety, abandonment, low self-esteem, lousy parenting, suicidal thoughts, and more. They walk the hallways trying to figure out how to be normal, but never receive answers.

I tell all of my students that Math is a metaphor for life. I will answer their Math problems as well as their life problems.

Every problem has an answer; we must find the person to teach us how to solve it.

Although you may not be a teenager anymore, a teenage version is buried in your subconscious that never had these problems answered. Now, you are living a depressed life because the teenager in you never got the answer on how to deal with depression.

This book is the answer to your teenage problems!

As we journey from hurting to healing, we will laugh, cry, and explore many different emotions. When we reach the end, we will have principles that will guide us for the rest of our lives.

This book isn't theory, and neither is it speculation. It is a proven formula that will answer the teenage problems you have swept under the rug.

Drawing on my real-life experiences, I have created cheat codes to guide you from hurt to healing. All you have to do is pick up the controller and enter the codes.

I have discovered life's algorithm, and although it shifts often, this book is the formula that'll keep you right in the middle.

You may read this book in a day, week, or month. No matter how long it takes you, I want to be the first to congratulate you for starting your journey from hurting to healing!

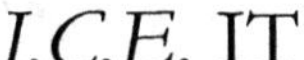

I.C.E. IT

—— **CHAPTER 1** ——

Put Some ICE On It

I remember playing basketball at school one day when I was a teenager. I went up for a rebound, fell, and hurt my knee. Immediately, inflammation kicked in, and I began to think, "God, please do not let this be an ACL, MCL, PCL, LCL, or anything else with an acronym."

They took me to the trainer, and she performed mobility tests and asked questions about how I got hurt. When she finished the tests and questions, she walked over to the ice machine, grabbed her big metal scooper, and put a mound of ice in a plastic bag. She twisted it, sucked the air out of it, and formed it so that it would sit on my knee. She placed the ice bag on my knee and explained that I would feel cold, burning, aching, and numbing. I asked her if I needed the ice because I hate the cold. She told me that those feelings were necessary for me to heal and that no ice meant no healing. Even though I had a disdain for cold objects, I reluctantly said ok, because I knew it was the fastest way to heal. Saying yes to the ice meant saying yes to the other feelings and emotions that came with it. I will never forget the last thing she said as I got ready to limp out of the room. She said, "When the inflammation goes down, we can identify what is wrong with your knee."

When it comes to our emotional and mental health, injuries, also known as traumas, are a bit different. Unlike physical injuries, mental and emotional injuries often go untreated for a few reasons.

The first reason is that we think we can get by limping or barely making it. We rationalize that what we are going through isn't that bad or that we can make it. If you have ever had a physical injury that caused immobility to any part of your body, you know that when one thing hurts, it will spread to something else! Other areas of your body will overcompensate for the one part that does not work. That is why taking the necessary steps to heal the injury is essential. The same thing applies to your mental health. You cannot bury your traumatic experience under the rug and think that it will not affect the other areas of your life.

The second reason is that we need to realize that the condition of our brains determines the quality of our lives on Earth. Suppose you are constantly irritated, frustrated, sad, mad, depressed, or anxious. If that's the case, it's likely because something deeper inside you is still hurting, and the emotions you're feeling now are actually rooted in past traumatic experiences.

The third reason is that culture does not promote mental health as much as it should. I cringe when I watch a show that stereotypes therapy down to an actor portraying a therapist who is disconnected, dull, or bitter. Therapy is not like that. Therapy is freeing, life-changing, and healing! I will dive into this more later in the book.

Similar to the knee, traumatic experiences are difficult to heal because they involve so many emotions. As emotional beings, one experience can trigger multiple emotions. Putting ice on your feelings will bring forth other emotions. Do not be so afraid of the emotions that you avoid the ice. Without *ICE*, you cannot heal.

CHAPTER 2

Identify the Hurt
Increasing Your Emotional Intelligence

Let's be honest, spending time in your brain reliving thoughts you don't want is scary. For 20 years, I did not think of my trauma. I was so numb to what happened to me that I did not realize that I was functioning in my hurt.

I now realize that I didn't tell anyone my secret because I didn't want the person who hurt me to face repercussions, and I didn't want anyone to look at me differently because of the type of hurt that I endured.

Can you imagine the emotions in my heart when I started to process this for the first time as a 28-year-old? I was sad because I wondered why I had to go through this. I was angry because I let the person go 20 years without saying anything. I was anxious because I knew I would have to tell my mom. Processing your trauma will lead to you examining your emotions. No matter how uncomfortable it may be, processing your trauma and analyzing your feelings are the first steps to unlocking your next level.

Emotional Intelligence

Healing requires you to identify your emotions and their effect on you. Everyone is born an emotional being, so being able to identify when you are experiencing emotions tied to hurt is a sign of emotional intelligence.

Emotional intelligence is the ability to put words to your emotions, which requires you to spend time with yourself. When you want to better understand your emotions, you will encounter situations that deepen your understanding of your inner self. Sometimes, these experiences are good, and other times, they are bad. We should study them by asking, "Why do I feel this way?" "What brought this emotion?" and "Do I like what I feel?" Take some time to sit in a quiet place, free of distractions, and pinpoint your emotions.

As a dad, I find it funny trying to figure out what is wrong with Deuce, my son. Whenever he comes to me experiencing what seems to be the worst thing ever for him, I have him take a deep breath, talk slower, and process what happened so that he can put an emotion on it. I have him use this sentence stem, "Daddy, I feel (emotion), because (what happened)."

Most of the time, Deuce tells me that he is experiencing an emotion that's in line with being mad. However, he can say mad in at least four different ways. He tells me he is angry, upset, frustrated, or irritated. While they are all similar, they each have a different meaning. When he tells me which word he feels, I can talk him through that emotion.

Learning different words to express your feelings, rather than generalizing with one or two words, enhances your ability to identify your feelings.

You are not a bad person because you get mad, frustrated, irritated, or angry. I used to wrestle with those emotions, thinking that I was tripping because I was experiencing a negative or unwanted emotion. I failed to realize that negative or unwanted emotions are a part of our human experience, and the more we fight them, the stronger they get in our heads.

What emotions are you supposed to show when you go through a divorce? What about when you lose a job or a loved one? These are all traumatic experiences that are supposed to produce unwanted emotions. Experiencing unwanted emotions such as grief, depression, anxiety, anger, or anything of the like fills our body with guilt and regret because we feel like happiness, joy, and peace are supposed to be the only emotions we feel.

Wanted or unwanted, the emotions you experience are unique to you. They are what make you, you! Your emotions are a part of your story, and dismissing them robs you of the bigger picture of your life.

On the one hand, you are experiencing so much hurt, pain, and shame because of what happened to you. On the other hand, you are probably telling yourself that you shouldn't be feeling this way and that you should stop crying because it's not that big of a deal.

The battle between wanted and unwanted emotions will lead to a war inside of you that produces stress, depression, self-hate, low self-esteem, and anxiety. These emotions stem from an internal battle between good and evil, and between right and wrong.

The Principle of Duality

On your journey from hurting to healing, you must learn the Principle of Duality. The principle states that it is okay to experience two emotions simultaneously, even though they are opposite.

How do you handle grief and good? What about anger and happiness? What about the pain of hurting and the pleasure of healing? Adopting the principle of duality in your life means accepting that you have two powerful forces inside of you that are warring daily.

When you embrace your duality, you can understand that you are not a bad person because you are experiencing unwanted and uncomfortable emotions. In fact, the inflammation of unwanted emotions means your body is trying to heal itself. When you start identifying everything that you feel, you will be able to heal.

Paul, the author of two-thirds of the books in the New Testament Bible, puts it this way, "I have discovered this principle of life—that when I want to do what is right, I inevitably do what is wrong. I love God's law with all my heart. But there is another power within me that is at war with my mind. This power makes me a slave to the sin that is still within me. Oh, what a miserable person I am! Who will free me from this life that is dominated by sin and death? Thank God! The answer is in Jesus Christ our Lord. So you see how it is: In my mind I really want to obey God's law, but because of my sinful nature I am a slave to sin."

In this text, we can see how Paul identified the war within him. He even thought of himself as a miserable person. By identifying and talking about what was happening in his head, Paul realized he could not be a slave to the war he was battling because Jesus had freed him.

You are no different than Paul. Jesus has freed you, too! It's ok to have unwanted emotions and thoughts. You are not a lesser person. You may think you are too damaged, but you have also been delivered. You have the choice of which one to focus on.

Identification Leads to Revelation

In 2022, Shundra, my wife, and I stayed in an apartment in Bedford, Texas. One Saturday afternoon, I walked into our garage and smelt a horrible stench, but I could not figure out what it was. I knew it was something dead. I immediately started looking for squirrels, raccoons, possums, and anything else that could produce such a foul stench. Later that evening, we went to run some errands, and when we got out of the car, the smell was still there! I began to think, "How is this smell following us?"

Turns out that the smell was coming from under her hood. I wondered, "What on earth is underneath her hood that can produce such a foul smell?" I popped the hood and, after inspecting it, noticed a dead pigeon under her motor. I know you're wondering how a pigeon got underneath her motor… Yeah, me too. The good news is that I was able to take it to a tire shop so they could lift the car, undo the plate at the bottom of her car, and remove the pigeon. When they uncovered the pigeon, it filled the whole area with a stench so foul that everyone had to stop working and get some fresh air.

The hurt in your life is just like this foul smell. It follows you everywhere you go and sometimes can be hard to identify. You find yourself wondering, "What's wrong with me?" or "Why do I feel this way?" You might ask, "Why do my relationships always seem unhealthy?" "Why am I not where I want to be in life?" or "Why does loss keep showing up in my story?" You slowly begin accepting a narrative of yourself that is based on hurt because you are unable to identify why the foul stench of hurt is following you wherever you go.

You are not the reason your life is producing a foul stench. Your trauma is! Your trauma has been dead, buried beneath other life events that you wouldn't think to search. It follows you wherever you go and can be smelled through your actions. You are asking all of these soul-searching questions when the truth of the matter is that you have buried a trauma so deep in your brain that you do not realize it is producing unwanted actions and situations.

By identifying your trauma, you are revealing your healing. Do not avoid that secret you haven't told anyone, because what lies underneath that secret is a life unimaginable!

Put The Work In

Throughout this book, I have included an interactive process to help you do what you learned in that chapter/section. The questions and promptings in *Put The Work In* will aid you on your journey from hurting to healing. These questions and action steps are what I did to journey from hurting to healing. Feel free to extend the exercises to where they are practical for you.

Please participate in these action steps by writing them down and taking action on what you write. Healing is intentional. Are you ready to put the work in?

Take a second to close your eyes and reflect on any life situation that has caused hurt in your life. Once you have thought of them, in the table below, write them down and explain how they have held you back. I have provided an example. (If the provided area is not enough, complete this exercise in a journal.)

Identify The Hurt:

Who/What has hurt you?	How has it held you back?
Ex: Growing up without a present father.	*Ex: I did not have the confidence I needed as a man.*

CHAPTER 3

Confess The Hurt
Grace, Power, and Confession

God wants you to heal. He is so powerful that he will take what is hurting you and use it to heal you. In 2 Corinthians 12:1-10, Paul talks about having a thorn in his flesh. He talks about a satanic thorn that was wearing him out. He pleaded with God three times to heal him by removing it, but God looked at it and decided to heal him by leaving it there. Even though Satan meant harm, God used what Satan meant for evil, blessed it, and turned it for good!

Paul actively participated in a paradigm shift by discussing what was hurting him. At first, what was hurting him was holding him down, but by confessing the hurt, God came in and gave him a new perspective on what he was going through.

There are two revelations that God told Paul, and He wants you to know them, too:

1. My grace is all you need.
2. My power works best in your weakness.

God's grace is what allows you to make it through. It keeps you from being consumed by everything you have faced and will face. His power enables you to produce fruit even when you are weak and tired. You need to talk about your thorn in the flesh to activate God's grace and power.

The thorn that has been a pain in your side will turn into your testimony that breathes life into other people. The pain in your heart that has held you down will become the foundation you now stand on. The trials that have slowed you down will become the fuel that keeps you going. Your testimony is not formed without a test. Your message is not created without mess. Do not conceal your hurt; confess.

These are my Confessions: Communicating your thorn is the first step to shifting from hurting to healing.

By definition, to confess means to communicate something to someone. Talking to others about what you are going through is hard. You feel like people will judge you and not understand you, or maybe you feel like they can't really understand. I get it. Confessing is hard, but it is a skill that will take you to a new level.

Confession requires two things:

1. It requires you to have someone whom you can confide in. Having the right person in your life to talk to is paramount to your shifting from hurting to healing. Culture has created the false narrative that says, "I'm ok" when you are not. You need someone who knows when you aren't okay, even when you feel like you are. I will discuss this further in a later chapter.

2. The second thing confession requires is transparency and vulnerability. Transparency is telling the truth when asked about something. Vulnerability is being

open about something not asked. What good does having someone to talk to but refuse to talk to them do?

I identified my trauma years ago, but I kept it a secret for two decades. I didn't discuss it with my mom or my friends. I pushed it so far back in my head that I forgot about it.

As a result of not talking about what happened to me, my trauma affected me as a high school and college student, employee, friend, husband, and father. I started to despise myself and adopted the mantra that all good things must come to an end. I didn't believe it was meant for me to live a good life. When I was going through life, I failed to realize that my trauma controlled my perspective. I began to always expect a favourable situation to end badly. My brain only knew hurt, so it produced hurt vision. I expected to be hurt.

I adopted the skill of confessing in 2022 when I had to tell my wife and my mom what happened to me two decades earlier. God had to remind me of my trauma when we were having an honest heart-to-heart about who I am.

One day in December of 2022, God revealed to me that it wasn't me; it was my trauma. He surgically walked me through how my trauma had led me to behave a certain way as a child and an adult. He told me that what happened to me as a little boy impacted my behavior as an adult. After he was done showing me the impact that my trauma had on my life, he shoved me into a conversation with my wife. I was reluctant because I knew this level of vulnerability would require me to be prepared to be transparent and answer the questions that followed.

I confessed to Shundra, my wife, that as a young boy, from the ages of 6-9, I was sexually abused. During this conversation, I felt two emotions at once. I was uncomfortable and also experiencing a sense of freedom. I felt light, and I also felt a wave of sad emotions. These emotions began because I had finally released my biggest secret. I'd be lying to you if I told you it was a good feeling, because it isn't. But on the other side of your confession is a new life you have never imagined.

Four months after talking to God, Shundra, and my therapist, I met Tiffany White, a writing coach who helped me begin my journey. I met Eric Thomas, the number one motivational speaker in the world. Jeremy Anderson, Eric Thomas' A1 from day one, baptized me in Atlanta, Georgia. Jared Scott, the national motivational speaker of the year, is now my brother, with whom I enjoy playing top golf. I even started a business called Coach Williams University that focuses on shifting people from hurting to healing by changing the way they think.

I don't list these things to boast or brag about because they happened only by God's grace and power. However, I list these to show you the fruits of my confession. My confession led to my next level, and your confession will lead to yours, too.

God promises you grace and power to get through it, but you must be willing to put the work in, too. His grace and power work best with your willingness to work, and most of your work will be just talking to your trusted people.

We learn a transforming lesson through Paul—God's grace and power come through your confession.

Put The Work In

Confess The Hurt:

Now that you have identified what has hurt you, write down who you can discuss with within the space provided.

Keep in mind that talking it through is more than a venting session. It is an intentional process that will provide growth when you speak to the right person.

Reflect on these questions to help you identify who you need to talk to:

1. Who has wisdom?

2. Who is a good listener?

3. Who is available?

4. Who gives excellent advice?

5. Who do I trust?

Name	Relationship

—— **CHAPTER 4** ——

Embrace Who You Are
You are not what you have been through

Mastering affection will lead to embracing your reflection.

The word embrace literally means to hold affectionately in your arms. Embracing who you are means simply being affectionate with yourself. Hold yourself tight. Think of yourself as worthy of your own attention and affection.

In February of 2023, we welcomed our second son, Champ, into this world. Seeing my second son being born was a moment that I will never forget.

I remember when we locked eyes for the first time. Champ was lying on a table, crying very loudly, right after he took his first breath. His head was shaking. His eyes were squeezed tightly as they were getting adjusted to the light. Once the nurses got done cleaning him, they swaddled him, picked him up, and placed him in my arms. I sang to him, and he eventually settled down within seconds. He looked at me, and I looked at him with the biggest smile on my face.

I remember the nurses telling me babies feel the most affection from skin-to-skin contact, so I took my shirt off and sat in a recliner. They placed him on my chest and left the room. Shundra was being cleaned up and wasn't in our room yet. It was just Champ and me. Father and son. Rocking ever so slowly, I held him snuggly, kissed his forehead, and sang Champion by Maverick City Music to him.

Can you remember the first time you held your child? If you don't have kids, what about your niece, nephew, or maybe a friend's baby? If you've never held a baby, imagine being comforted by a person you love in a very unfamiliar territory while you experience emotions that you've never felt before.

To embrace who you really are, you must learn the skill of showing yourself affection. I'm talking about the same affection you would show a newborn baby. What does embracing yourself look like to you?

For me, I have affirmations listed by my bathroom mirror that I look at every day. Affirmations like "I am a good father" and "I am a good husband" create the foundation of who I am. I also affirm who I will be because who I will be is who I am now – I have to wait a little bit to become. Before I finished this book, I told myself I am an author. When I am having a bad day, I tell myself I will make it through.

When you look in the mirror, you have to see that there's still a newborn baby in you who needs to be shown affection. You deserve to be held. You deserve to be looked at like it's the first time you've ever been seen! You deserve to be loved!

Emotions Make You Cry Sometimes

Emotions can make you cry, and they can make you laugh. Emotions can make you feel euphoric, but they can also make you feel pain.

If you could make a list of the top five emotions that you experience in a day, week, or month, what would they be? If you're like me, emotional, I'm sure it was hard to get them down to just five.

Regardless of what you listed or how many you listed, experiencing emotions is entirely normal. They are unique to you.

Emotions make you who you are meant to be.

I remember when I stayed in Denver for a little while. Staying there was transformational for me, because I learned so much about my makeup as a man by experiencing what felt like an army of emotions.

When we decided to move there, I was supposed to work for the Arvada Police Department and as the Connections Pastor of a church up there. Shundra was going to stay at home to take care of Deuce.

We were going to live our best life in Downtown Denver. Our apartment was two blocks from Coors Field, one mile from the Denver Nuggets arena, and two miles from Mile High Stadium–home of the Denver Broncos.

One month before we moved to Denver, I received an email notifying me that I didn't get the police job. I was devastated and disappointed, but at the same time, I was determined to obey the word I heard from God. I'll get into this later in the book, though.

Can you imagine the bundle of emotions that I felt when it started to sink in that I did not have a way to provide for my family?

I felt anxiety, anger, frustration, disappointment, and nervousness. It was like a tidal wave of emotions that hit all at once.

I suppressed most of these emotions because I knew I had to be strong for my family. What I didn't understand at that time was that you can be strong and show emotions at the same time. This experience taught me that showing emotions is a sign that I am strong and working correctly.

In life, you will be given a series of tests that will solicit emotions and give you a deeper understanding of who you are. Do not fight them. Dissect them. Get to know them better because your emotions aren't going anywhere.

All emotions are natural responses to your internalization of the situations you face. When dealing with my emotions, I learned not to fight them because fighting something that will keep showing up is pointless and will leave you in a dark place.

When you feel wanted and unwanted emotions, stop and identify what brought those emotions to the surface. Communicate with yourself about how they made you feel and what they made you think about. When you get into the habit of identifying and communicating your emotions, it will become much easier to embrace who you are.

Embracing who you are begins with you embracing who you are inside.

You are not what you have been through

Embracing who you are is understanding that you are not what you have been through. Stop living through the lens of what has hurt you and live through the lens of who God created you to be.

Focus on the impact you want to leave on this Earth. Think about the legacy that will remain on Earth once you are no longer here. Your kids. Your namesake. Your business. Your wealth.

Life comes with its fair share of issues. The most vital stories are the ones that have been through fire! Your experiences are unique to you, and it's up to you to see yourself as the loved creation that you are.

Time has three moments. The past, the present, and the future. The past is what happened to you and who you were. The present is how you handle what happened to you and who you currently are. The future is what can happen for you and who you want to be.

No matter where you are in your life, what is ahead of you will always be far greater than what is in your past. You have to decide now, in the present, that you do not want your future version to be held down by past experiences and emotions.

I get it. Life happens, and some of the things you go through are out of your control. The one thing you can control is your perception of yourself as you go through the ups and downs of life.

On your journey, discipline yourself to focus on what lies ahead, not on what lies behind. You can't run a race looking behind you the whole time. You run with the end goal in mind. Paul puts it this way in Philippians 3:13-14, "I focus on this one thing: Forgetting the past and looking forward to what lies ahead. I press on to reach the end of the race and receive the heavenly prize for which God, through Christ Jesus, is calling us."

The past is the past, and the future is the future. Which one do you want to control your life?

Embracing who you are means embracing who God created you to be, your future, and the journey towards healing. Always remember that you are not what you have been through.

Put The Work In

Embrace Who You Are: There have been things in your life that have hurt you, which is perfectly fine! You are normal! In the space provided below, list three or more things you love about yourself– Affirmations.

1. ____

2. ____

3. ____

Now, write down a list of emotions that you struggle with. As you write them down, remember that emotions mean you work normally!

1. ____

2. ____

3. ____

Be *S.T.I.L.L.*

CHAPTER 5

Silence The Noise
Be Still So You Can Heal

When I was 12 years old, I was playing a Little League baseball game when my knee suddenly gave out. I remember it like it was yesterday.

I was on the Mariners, and we were playing the Astros for first place! It was the bottom of the 6th inning. The Astros were leading 7 to 6, and we needed a run to tie it up and send it to extra innings. I walked up to the plate, knowing that my team needed me on base as the leadoff hitter.

I was facing the best pitcher, and he was pitching to the fastest 12-year-old in the league. He threw a knuckleball, and I hit a dribbler down the first base line. As I ran to first base as fast as possible, I noticed the first baseman bobbling the ball because I was coming so fast. Eventually, he picked up the ball and stepped on the base.

As I was nearing first base and the first baseman was getting ready to step on the bag, I fell out of nowhere, immediately grabbing my knee.

With my team looking on in disbelief and the crowd gasping for air, wondering if I was ok, my coach picked me up and carried me to my mom's white Intrepid.

She rushed me to the emergency room, where I waited for what seemed to be all night long. Finally, I saw the doctor, and he told me that I was suffering from what is called tendonitis—something that most teenagers and athletes go through.

Along with inflammation medicine, he gave me exercises to strengthen my knee. He told me I would heal if I stayed off my knee and remained still.

Through this experience comes a vital life lesson. If you want to shift from hurting to healing, you must learn how to be still to heal.

Over the next few chapters, you will learn how to be *STILL* so that you can heal. You will be equipped with information that will teach you how to *Silence* the noise, make *Time*, be *Intentional*, *Love* yourself, and *Lock* in.

Silence the Noise

Whatever has your attention controls your ascension. Noise can be defined as something or someone that has your attention. Noise is negative, weighs you down, and prevents you from hearing logic.

While noise can take many forms, it can be broken down into three categories: People, Media, and Mindset. Let's take a look at these three things.

Noisy People

Have you ever met someone who is always negative? They never talk about goals, vision, or life improvement. This is the person to whom you really do not look forward to speaking with.

These people leave you drained after conversing with them, with no energy to take care of yourself.

The first step in being *STILL* is to silence the noise coming from people's mouths! There are people in your life who are just way too loud! They have too much influence over you!

Unfortunately, the noisiest people can be the ones closest to you. People like your mom, dad, friends, and even your significant other. While their intentions are good, they cause weight in your life because they are talking to you from a heavy place of hurt.

So what do you do if you have noisy people in your life? Create personal boundaries.

Boundaries are lines that people can not cross. You must stick with them when you create them because people will cross them if they aren't defined and strong.

I hate arguing. It disturbs my peace. I remember my last argument and how it made me feel. I left the argument wondering what in the world am I doing? It drained me. I had emotions flying all over the place. I decided to stop arguing because there was no need to forcefully explain myself to the point that I was thrown off my rocker.

Like me, I am sure you have had arguments with your mom, dad, siblings, and with the person you are dating or married to. Can you reflect on how you felt after those arguments? After every argument is an emotion. You may leave that argument crying, mad, sad, depressed, anxious, or all in one!

Because of these draining emotions, I do not argue anymore. That's a boundary that I set that no one can cross. I am vocal with this boundary, no matter who the person is. If two adults can't sit and exchange opinions without tempers flaring, they are not in a healthy relationship.

Creating a personal boundary around arguing is one of the many ways I have shifted from hurting to healing. My mental health is more important than winning an argument. Besides, what is the quality of my circle if I am constantly arguing with them?

Noisy Media

We live in a world where the influence of social media is rising exponentially. People post highlights of their lives, riches, and relationships, inspiring and influencing others to live just like them.

The problem with this is that on the other side of the screen are unrealistic expectations that leave us feeling empty because we so deeply desire someone else's lifestyle. It is easy to get lost in the noise of social media and to want a life lived by others, not one that is purposed for you.

While there's no problem manifesting material things, the noise comes in when you manifest something you are unwilling to work for.

You manifest a romantic marriage, but can't be faithful to one person. You manifest millions, but don't make time to expand your financial means. You manifest big houses, but spend your money on vain things.

Manifesting other people's realities creates a false mindset of where you think you need to be. This creates an endless cycle of anxiety and depression because you are in the middle of a big dream but living in a less-than-ideal reality.

What people post is not the measure of your life. It's just noise because they show you the fruits of their labor, but not the hard work or the inheritance that got them there.

Stop setting expectations for goals that you did not set. Stop desiring someone else's reality and put the work into creating your own.

Silencing social media means you spend less time scrolling and posting and more time working and creating.

Noisy Mindset

The fastest way to transform your life is not by actually changing your life; it is, however, by changing your mind. Your life goes wherever your mind is.

Romans 12:2 says that you should let God transform you into a new person by changing the way you think. How you think is critical to whether or not you start a new life of healing. It doesn't matter how many degrees you have, how many businesses you have started, or how many books you have written. God wants to constantly change the way you think. There's always room to level up your brain!

I remember the Chick-fil-A commercial where a guy was on his way to work and kept eating the same breakfast sandwich. He eventually looked up and noticed he was in a rut because what he ate did not match what Chick-fil-A had to offer. His mind was so fixed on his routine that he thought he was in a groove, but a co-worker pointed out that it was actually a rut.

Like Chick-fil-A, what God has to offer you is so much better than what you are currently digesting. Comfortability and complacency have you stuck in a mental rut because you are used to your routine and will not venture outside. Stop repeating behaviors that leave you in a rut. God wants you to live a healthy life, and he has prepared things that you should set your mind on.

God wants to change how you think about finances, relationships, and jobs, but he can not do that until you allow him to change how you think about yourself.

If you think you are destined to live a life of hurt, then it will be so, but if you have faith and believe you can heal, it will be so! To transform into a healthy person, you need to let God change the way you think.

Silencing the noise around you is paramount to your healing journey. People will not agree with the decisions you make, but so what? There has to come a point in your life where you stop caring what people think about you.

Those closest to you won't understand what you are doing because they haven't experienced it.

When you decide to heal, you choose to break generational curses. When you start breaking generational curses, chains will break, eyes will lift, and mouths will open. You do not have to live in the hurt that those before you have. Do what it takes to silence the noise in your life. Your next level is waiting for you.

Put The Work In

Noisy People:

1. Who are the noisy people in your life?

   a. ____

   b. ____

   c. ____

2. What are they saying?

   a. ____

   b. ____

   c. ____

3. What are the boundaries you can set up to silence the noise?

   a. ____

   b. ____

   c. ____

Noisy Media:

1. Take a minute to check your phone's screen time.

    a. <u>iPhone</u>: Settings > Screen Time

    b. <u>Android</u>: Settings > Digital Wellbeing > Dashboard > Screen Time

2. What social media apps do you spend the most time on?

    a. _______________________________

    b. _______________________________

    c. _______________________________

3. In what ways have these apps influenced you?

    a. _______________________________

    b. _______________________________

    c. _______________________________

4. Write down your plan to silence social media noise.

    ____

    ____

    ____

Noisy Mindset:

1. List 3 unhealthy things that you think about.

    a. ____

    b. ____

    c. ____

2. List 3 healthy things that you should start thinking about

    a. ____

    b. ____

    c. ____

3. Why is it essential to switch your mindset?

    ____

    ____

    ____

    ____

CHAPTER 6

Make *TIME*
You Are The Most Important Person

Healing requires you to make time, not find time. You have to make time for things that are not a natural part of your day until they become a consistent habit.

God will do exceedingly abundantly above everything that you can ask or think, according to the power that works in you! You just have to make the time for it. Make time to do what brings healing to your life.

I do not doubt your desire to heal; however, I do question your tenacity to make the time to do so. How much depression is too much? When is enough, enough? At what point will you become sick and tired of being sick and tired? When will you decide to stop worrying about what will not matter tomorrow?

Your inability to make time for what makes you healthy has kept you in a mindset of hurt. God has given you 24 hours in a day to steward over. You can create a schedule that prioritizes you and your health.

I understand that kids, 12-hour work shifts, and all of life's other responsibilities make it hard to find time, but you can never live your best life feeling suboptimal in your mind.

It is not fair to you to give your all to someone else's vision and your leftovers to yours. You are the most important person in your life. This is why it's important to make time for yourself.

I bet you are wondering, "How on earth can I make time when I do not have time?" That is a great question. Let's observe how Jesus did it.

In Matthew 14, we see Jesus make time for himself by going away alone to pray. The first instance was because he was grieving the death of his cousin, John. The second was after he fed 5,000 people.

We can also find in Matthew 26 that Jesus went away from everyone else to pray. Jesus made it his priority to make time for himself. Most of the time, it was early in the morning or late at night, because the middle of the day was so busy for him.

Is healing important enough for you to wake up one hour earlier than normal? If you're not a morning person, what about staying up one hour later? What about on your days off? How are you spending the time that you do have?

God has given you 24 hours in a day and 168 hours in a week. It is up to you to make time in your schedule for what matters the most. If you are unfamiliar with what matters the most, then let me remind you– YOU DO! You matter the most!

Regardless of whether you wake up early or stay up late, it will not be easy starting off. Stay disciplined, and do not get discouraged. Remember, if it were easy, then everyone would do it.

Five Exercises That You Should Make Time For

When you want to heal, you will make time to do it. Here is a list of 5 exercises you should make time for.

1. **Go on a morning or evening walk.** Not only is walking physically healthy, but it is also spiritually healthy. God loves to walk and talk with you and will often give you life-changing revelations when you slow down and walk with him. We often get caught up in the trials of life that we do not even realize that we are running 90 to nothing! Make time in your day to slow everything down and focus.

2. **Journal everyday**. For me, journaling is a time when I can express myself. I can write down what I am feeling, good or bad. I can write out my prayers or even write down my visions. There is not only one way to journal, so just write until you find your niche. If you are not used to writing, it can be tough to get started. Like anything else, give yourself time and set journaling goals. But first, go buy a journal! It will change your life.

3. **Read your Bible**. I know, I know… You don't read the bible because it has been misused, the scriptures have been taken out of context and used as weapons, and it was used to support slavery. Maybe the King James Version is just too hard for you to understand. Whatever the reason is why you do not read, God is

telling you right now to erase that mindset. He wants you to give him another try!

Find a version of the bible that you like and understand. There are many credible versions like the English Standard Version (ESV), the New International Version (NIV), and the New American Standard Bible (NASB). I personally read the New Living Translation (NLT). Go to a bookstore near you, or download a Bible app, read a couple of scriptures in each version, and choose the one you like best. You may already have your bible, but do not know where to start. I suggest that you start with John, because John was written so that you will believe in Jesus (John 20:31). It is by that belief that you will have life. If you are tired of hurting, and want a new life of healing, start reading the gospel of John.

4. **Go to therapy**. I will expound on this in much more detail in a later chapter, but what God wants you to know now is that you need to let go of your stigma about therapy. Culture and media have painted a false view of what therapy really is. Whenever you are experiencing pain, where do you go? The doctor, right? You know that the doctor can prescribe the right medicine and run the correct tests in order to diagnose you and send you on a journey of healing. In that same way, a therapist can run the right tests and suggest medicine for you, if needed. Do not fall into the stigma

of not telling people your business. A therapist is not an ordinary person. He/she is a trained, certified brain healer. Make time for therapy at least once a month.

5. **Find your chair**. A chair is something that you do for yourself. It is where you sit down and slow down. It is a time when you relax and take care of yourself. Whenever I feel stressed or overwhelmed, I play Madden or barbecue. When I sit in my chair, nothing else matters besides what is right in front of me. I do not think about work, stress, depression, anxiety, anger, or anything of that nature. I simply sit and enjoy my own company. You may not be able to do this every day, and that is fine, but it needs to be a part of your weekly schedule. Make time, one day out of the week, to sit in your chair. Once it becomes part of your routine, make it 3-4 times a week. Eventually, you want to practice some form of self-care every day.

The quality of your life depends on your physical, mental, and emotional health. Make time in your daily, weekly, and monthly schedule to prioritize all facets of your health.

Put The Work In

1. In the table below, create a time map of how you currently spend your day. Track your time from when you wake up to when you go to sleep. Include work, personal care, prayer time, etc. Do not leave a detail off. Feel free to create this in your journal if you run out of room.

Time	Task

2. Now, I want you to create a time map of your ideal day. If you could add anything, add it; if you can take anything away, take it away.

Time	Task

3. Consider these questions:

    a. What are the differences between your current day and your ideal day?

    b. Is there anything you can take away from your current day to add to your ideal day?

    c. What is your strategy to make time for healing?

— **CHAPTER 7** —

Be *INTENTIONAL*

What Is Filling You Up Determines How Far You Go

Being *STILL* requires you to be intentional with your pour. Be mindful of prioritizing other people over yourself. When you take care of other people without taking care of yourself, you will eventually start pouring from an empty cup. Pouring from an empty cup leads to burnout, fatigue, and a loss of purpose.

In 2019, I was a teacher, coach, and pastor– three very draining careers. My life was centered on filling other people's cups while often neglecting my own. Who did I have pouring into me at the rate that I was pouring into others?

I was pouring into other people with an empty cup! It was a draining time for my family and me. I was easily irritated and frustrated, and thought that it was just who I was. I lost sight of my purpose and got lost in the desires of the world. I was a beaming light for others, but had darkness within me. The world saw a smile; my family saw brokenness. I isolated myself and just figured that the feelings would pass if I smiled enough.

Satan is a coward and will come for you at your weakest time. He prowls around like a roaring lion, looking for someone to devour. When lions hunt for food, their objective is to isolate the prey from the herd and attack it. Satan, like a lion, wants to do the same to you. When you are empty and going through the ups and downs of life, do not isolate.

When God created the heavens and the earth, the only thing that was not good was for man to be alone. When you are alone, Satan will show you the alcohol bottle. When you are alone, he will tempt you with porn. When you are alone, he will come in, pick you apart, and fill you up with things that disconnect you from your purpose. This is why it is important to be intentional about who and what you fill yourself with.

What's Filling You Up?

Have you ever gotten gas that burned out quickly? No matter how slow you drive, or how much you limit your driving radius, it still burns out! That's probably because you put some bad gas into your tank. A car that is filled with bad gas will burn out faster. If you keep putting that bad gas into your car, it will eventually start to mess up other parts under the hood. The only way to rectify your car from burning out of gas too fast is to change your gas station!

Your life is exactly the same. Bad gas is anything that is not in alignment with God's will for your life. Who you listen to on TikTok or YouTube matters. What you talk about in your friend groups matters. Who you are dating matters. If you keep allowing toxic gas in your life, you will never elevate. You cannot operate at the capacity God created you for with bad gas in your tank.

Bad gas in your life could lead to burnout, loss of purpose, anxiety, depression, anger, bad decisions, fatigue, irritability, unhappiness, and more! Which would you rather do: live your life with bad gas, or change what's filling you up? I hope you want to change what's filling you up.

Once you replace the bad gas with good gas, your life will begin to run smoothly. Things will begin to line up. Blessings will begin to flow. You'll experience less drama. You will be able to go further in life. Gas matters!

Be Intentional

Your journey from hurting to healing depends on the type of gas that is in your life. Do not be filled with the superficial things of the world that will burn you out. Instead, be filled with the spirit of God! Read your bible. Listen to Christian principled podcasts. Listen to Christian music. Find a YouTube Pastor and listen to one sermon per week. You could even set reminders in your phone to pray more.

Being intentional is not easy, but it is important. You have to create new habits, listen to new people, and even change your friend groups. Intentionality will lead you to the next level in your life. You have to be intentional about what you put into your life and who you let influence you. Your journey from hurting to healing depends on how intentional you are.

Put The Work In

1. Below, identify the bad gas in your life. Think about your friends, family, music, and social media.

   a. ____

   b. ____

   c. ____

2. What are some good things that you are filling yourself up with?

   a. ____

   b. ____

   c. ____

3. Why is it important to fill up with good gas instead of bad gas?

   ____

   ____

   ____

4. What will you do to replace the bad gas with the good
    gas?

____

____

____

____

$$\text{———— CHAPTER 8 ————}$$

LOVE Yourself
Finding Your Gift

Before you begin reading this section, I want you to participate in an exercise. Grab your journal, or a piece of paper, and write down five things you love about yourself (i.e- hair, skin tone, height, talents, etc.). Was it hard for you to do this? Awkward, maybe? If you struggled with this exercise, then it is possible that your self-love is low. If you do not value yourself, how can you get the most out of your time here on earth?

Loving who you are is a pivotal piece in living a healed life. Life is too short to walk around hating yourself. Do not waste your time trying to change what you can't. Change what you can change, and embrace what you can't change. In fact, what you do not like about yourself is what God has given you to impact the world.

For most of my life, I hated my voice. Everywhere I went, people would mock my voice by making theirs deep and Kermit the frog-ish. What they didn't know was that by trying to imitate my voice, they were planting seeds of self-hate in my head. I started to hate my voice and didn't value it. Now, I know that my voice is my greatest gift!

My voice has taken me on a tour of London, singing in front of many iconic places, such as York Minster Cathedral,

London Bridge, and Edinburgh Castle. My voice has taken me to New York City to sing in Carnegie Hall. Most importantly, though, my voice has been used to transform lives in Jesus' name!

I had to realize that what people mocked, God made! My voice has put me in rooms that most people will never be in. It has given me a platform that most people desire. My voice is a gift from God that he gave me!

Do not hate the gift that God has given you! You think that you don't fit in, when in all actuality, you stick out! You have a gift from God that makes you stick out! If you have trouble finding it, it is probably the thing you hate the most!

I want you to participate in another exercise. Write down 5 things that you do not like about yourself. Place them into two categories. The first category is things that you can't change. For example, your voice, your facial features, your height, your body build, your past experiences, or your family.

The second category is things that you can change. For example, your weight, mindset, values, and habits. Make a plan to change what you can, and change your mindset about what you can't.

We apply the Serenity Prayer in other situations, but I would like for you to recite it with yourself in mind.

"God, grant me the serenity to accept the things I cannot change, the courage to change the things I can, and the wisdom to know the difference."

Put The Work In

1. Write down 5 things you love about yourself.

    a. ____

    b. ____

    c. ____

    d. ____

    e. ____

2. In the table below, write 5 things you can change about yourself, and in the other column write 5 things you can't change.

Can Change	Can't Change
1.	1.
2.	2.
3.	3.
4.	4.
5.	5.

3. What plan do you need to put in place to change what
    you can?

    50

    ____

    ____

    ____

    ____

4. Why is it important to fix your mindset on what you can't
    change about yourself?

    ____

    ____

    ____

    ____

CHAPTER 9

LOCK In
Standing On Business

Being locked into the healing process is important because many ugly, unwanted situations and emotions will come to the surface.

When I committed myself to healing, Satan got angry. I was presented with situations that were intended to derail me from my purpose. Satan didn't want me to heal because he knew that the more I healed, the more dangerous I was to his kingdom.

The same applies to you. Like a coach wanting to devise a scheme against his opponent, Satan watches film on your life, creating schemes that will keep you from even wanting to heal.

I can recall driving in Dallas down Highway 80, and was about to merge onto I-30 when I heard Satan say, "If you stop healing and serve me, then I will take away your anxiety, but if you continue down the path of healing, then I will make your life a living hell."

I immediately froze. I had never heard the voice of Satan so clearly. He started bringing up times in my life when I was in clubs and lounges, living my best life. He reminded me of seasons where I was living outside of my purpose. He wanted me to see that I was having "fun", and offered that life back to me.

In life, you will always have a choice between being locked into Satan's schemes or being locked into God's plan. To the eye, what Satan presents is glamorous, but it will lead to destruction. God's plan goes deeper than the eye and requires you to go through some things in order to get to the promise. Don't be locked into the wrong thing because you don't want to go deeper.

The Streets Keep You From Standing On Business

Living in the streets is a colloquial expression that could mean a few things. It could mean that you enjoy nightlife, are a hustler, like to have sneaky links, or it could even mean that you are in search of a good time— whatever that consists of.

I believe that streets are schemes of Satan that prevent you from locking into your next level.

Nightlife, lounges, drugs, alcohol, and scratching a sexual itch can be fun, but what do they do for your soul? Getting wasted to the point where you do not remember what happened may be funny to you, but it is very dangerous when you think about it. You're leaving yourself in a position to be taken advantage of without even remembering what happened.

What about linking up with a person you met at the club, and you don't even know them? You are trusting yourself with a person who you just met, all for the sake of fulfilling a desire.

Satan is clever. He presents you with the streets to prevent you from standing on business. He wants you to think that just because you secure the bag Monday through Friday, you should celebrate in the streets on the weekend.

These streets are the antithesis of what it means to stand on business, because they only provide you with temporary fulfillment. You constantly crave the next thing, the next high, the next drink, the next link, because the streets are not designed to fill you up long term. They are designed to be a temporary reprieve from a long week of work.

The streets distract you from locking in and healing. The time you spend in these streets is time you can spend writing your book, starting your business, or spending time with your children.

I understand that you may not be interested in the streets of nightlife, but I do believe there is a street distracting you from healing. What is your street?

Lock In With God

When you are presented with the option of what to be locked into, ask yourself this question: "Is what I am doing in alignment with the Spirit that lives in me?" If it is not, it's from Satan. If it is, it's from God. Remember that Satan is a deceiver and will twist the word of God. That's why it is important to stay in relationship with God!

Pray for an increase in capacity so that you can understand more fully the plans and promises of God! Do not be fooled by the superficial glamor of these streets. Lock in! Stand on business.

Remember that when you make the decision to lock into a relationship with God, Satan will present you with vices that distract you and prevent you from locking in and focusing. Do not be distracted by things that will derail your journey to healing; instead, stand on business. If you haven't figured it out yet, healing is your business.

What God has for you is far greater than anything Satan can offer you. By making the decision to lock in, you are building the path for generations after you to follow!

Put The Work In

1. Make a list of 5 ways you can lock in with God (i.e- read your bible)

    a. ____

    b. ____

    c. ____

    d. ____

    e. ____

2. Now, make a list of 5 things that will prevent you from locking in.

    a. ____

    b. ____

    c. ____

    d. ____

    e. ____

The Journey

CHAPTER 10

The Voice of God
How Does He Speak To You?

If God asked you today to pack up your family in 90 days and move 15 hours away, on His word alone, would you do it? Did you start thinking about other factors, like where you would work, where you would stay, how you would afford the move, and your kids' schooling?

Moving is already a hassle, but moving to a different state with different beliefs and vibes is tough. Few people would move on the drop of a dime with no real clarity.

Is your faith strong enough to do this? Mine was.

In August of 2020, while I was on the porch at a beautiful pastor's retreat in Coushatta, Louisiana, God spoke to me and said that He wanted me to move from Marshall, Texas, to Denver, Colorado. I had just turned 25 in July; Shundra, my wife, was 26; and Deuce, my son, had just turned 1.

Before I get into the details of the move and my time in Denver, I want to detail the conversation between God and me when he told me to pack up everything and move my family 15 hours away to a place I had never been.

The Unknown: When Life Is Life-ing

Before God told me to move to Denver in August 2020, I was going through my mid-20s crisis. I had been married for five years. Deuce was one year old, and we lived in a small city named Marshall, Texas. I had been in education for 5 years and had been a Lead Pastor for about 3 years. I was only 25 years old.

To say that I was busy is an understatement. If it wasn't family or school, then it was church. At that point in my life, I spent more time with others than with myself and my family.

If you know anything about teaching and pastoring, you know that they are underappreciated professions that have to jump through hurdles to better the lives of others. We have to spend time we don't have teaching others what they don't know while being underpaid.

On top of the regular hustle and bustle of teaching and pastoring, COVID-19 swept the world, forcing industries like education and the church to change how they did things.

As a 25-year-old man building my family and my quality of life, it was a massive thing for me. There were many questions I would ask myself quite often, summarized by this one: Is what I am making worth the time I spend away from my family?

To give you a little context, I made $48k teaching and coaching, and $400/month as a pastor. Yea… I know. That ain't enough money to build a family. We were living paycheck to paycheck with no room to save. While we were grateful to be able to pay our bills, we always worried about our future and if this was what our lives were going to be made of.

To add to this worry, I was going through a personal situation that required lawyers and the potential of a court case, while I was doing all that I was.

If anxiety had a door to walk through, this would definitely have been it. Anxiety is when you worry about something with an uncertain outcome.

I did not know what the future held for my family. I did not know how I would make more money. I did not know how my personal issues would pan out.

To sum it up, there were many unknowns in my life, and I did not know how to handle them.

Divine Direction: Abbie Lane Retreat Center

COVID-19 began to really shift America in the Spring of 2020. I remember leaving school for spring break and not returning for the rest of the school year.

Over the ensuing months, quarantine became a huge thing. The CDC was forced to create guidelines that instructed what to do if we came down with COVID-19. These guidelines governed how we grocery shopped, pumped gas, and entertained ourselves. Businesses were closed, schools were shut down, and loved ones were lost. We were forced into a long period of what we call quarantine.

Quarantine was a time of complete isolation. It was a time when we were around no one but our families. We even had to learn to be human again— as if it wasn't challenging the first time.

It was during this time that I was having my mid-20s crisis. Enough was enough. I was tired, frustrated, and anxious. Something had to give.

I decided to take my cue from COVID and metaphorically quarantine myself by going on a fast. A fast is a period of time when you go without something you need or desire to dedicate yourself to hearing from God. Some people fast from food, while others fast from watching TV or something of the like.

I decided to fast from sweets, sodas, and social media. My goal was to pray and seek God's discernment on what He wanted us to do with our future. Whenever I wanted to eat sweets, drink a soda, or get on social media, I prayed and meditated on what God wanted me to do.

A few days later, my spirit was led to search on Google for a "free pastors retreat near me." I ran across a few that weren't too expensive. I continued searching and eventually landed on The Abbie Lane Retreat Center in Coushatta, Louisiana, just 1.5 hours away. I looked at their website, and the retreat was free and legit, so I booked it for a week at the end of August 2020.

Although the website looked great, I had no idea what to expect when I arrived. Are the hosts friendly? How new are the cabins? Will I be eaten by alligators– since this is Louisiana we are talking about? Most importantly, will I be in a safe place?

I remember driving through the Louisiana woods, heading to Abbie Lane, wondering if I was on the right track! I was surrounded by swamp-like trees, roadkill all over the road, and vultures in the sky. "Lord, please lead me in the right direction," I thought.

My GPS eventually prompted me to turn left. As soon as I turned down the driveway, I felt God's presence! I was greeted by pine trees and acres and acres of land! I was nervous and didn't know what to expect from my stay, but I expected God to direct my path.

While at Abbie Lane, I stayed in a small cabin called The Father's House. Staying in The Father's House was the first sign I needed to see! It was a sign of promise, letting me know that God, my father, would tell me what to do while I was here.

God Speaks Through Everyday Things

Have you ever been so desperate for an answered prayer that you prayed the same words over and over again? Have you ever gone through a situation that required you to tap into God's voice?

When you are searching for answers from God, look for signs and listen to His voice. Do not mystify the voice of God by thinking that He has this low, thunderous voice. In my experience, I have never heard a James Earl Jones voice from heaven, as the clouds lit up, leaving rays beaming on my face. However, God will speak to you through familiar voices.

I believe He speaks through the Bible, others, and his creation. He will speak through everyday, simple things that you are familiar with. He wants us to hear him, so He will always make it plain. We don't have to travel through a never-ending maze to find his voice. We have to be in relationship with him, and we will hear His voice.

The conscience is an inner voice that guides us in making decisions. Our conscience is what God uses to speak to us; therefore, the stronger our relationship with God, the more clearly we hear Him in our heads and through everyday things.

Media, culture, and religion have unintentionally raised us to think that only the pastor or clergy can hear God's voice, but you can hear from God, too! If God can speak to Moses through a burning bush, He can speak to you!

The question is, will you recognize His voice when He speaks?

God Doesn't Make Empty Promises

During my stay at The Father's House, God led me to Genesis 12:1-3. In this passage of scripture, we are introduced to Abraham. God directed Abraham to leave his country, culture, and family and go to the land He would show him.

In The Father's House, the cabin I was staying in at Abbie Lane Retreat Center, God spoke to me clearly in a way I had never heard Him before. Every morning for three days straight, I woke up, sat on the porch, and read Genesis 12:1-3.

Through Genesis 12, God gave me five promises. I didn't understand them or agree with everything, so I sat on the porch every morning conversing with God, asking him honest questions about every word He gave me.

In the next chapter, I will break down the promises God and I discussed while I was at Abbie Lane.

—— CHAPTER 11 ——

Unpacking God's Voice
Obedience and Faith Unlocks God's Promises

One morning, as the winds blew and the thin Louisiana pine trees bent back and forth, I was sitting on the porch of The Father's House, my Abbie Lane cabin, reading Genesis 12:1-3. From these three verses, God decided to speak to me.

I remember calling Shundra and telling her what God was telling me. It was weird because I had never heard him so clearly before. I didn't even have to leave the first verse to hear what He was telling me.

In Genesis 12:1, God told Abraham to leave his native country, his relatives, and his father's family. Right then, I heard God tell me to move to Denver.

When I heard Him tell me to move to Denver, I looked up and saw the pine trees moving back and forth. At that moment, God said these words to me, "Just as the wind is blowing hard enough to move the trees, I have sent the Holy Spirit to move you."

The crazy thing is that up until this moment, I hadn't heard from God this clearly. Not only did He speak through my conscience, but He also spoke through his creation.

I was amazed, astonished, and apprehensive. It was almost like God knew I would be apprehensive, so He prepared five promises to reassure me that He had my back.

Promise 1: I Will *Make* You Into A Great Nation

In verse two of Genesis 12, God told Abraham, "I will make you into a great nation." My spirit stopped me right there.

I began praying and asking God how he was going to make me into a great nation. I mean, at that time, I only had one son, I was young, and figured no one would listen to me. Is this really for me, or was this specifically for Abraham?

Since then, I have added two kids to my family, and God is still giving me clarity on how he is making me into a great nation. At the time that He told me this, I took it literally, but now I know what He meant.

Faith is believing in what He tells you, even when it doesn't make sense to you. One thing is for sure: when God makes you a promise, it will come to pass; you just have to wait for his timing.

Promise 2: I Will *Bless* You

As I was sitting in the rocking chair on the porch, God told me to count all the pine straws on the ground.

I said, "God, it's too many."

He said, "Move to Denver, and my blessings for you will be too many to count."

Even as I type this, I am speechless because I can now reflect on the blessings that He has given me since He promised this, and there have definitely been too many to count.

Promise 3: I Will *Make* You Famous

Everyone wants to be famous in this culture, but in this season, all I wanted was rest! Fame did not entice me. I just wanted to chill with Shundra and Deuce and be left alone.

Aside from that, I asked God how I would even be famous? I don't like myself, so why would others like me?

My mind is all over the place. I don't have anything to offer anyone! Even if I did, I needed more to be famous! I asked God, "Is this for me, or do I need to bypass this?"

Years later, here I am, writing books, creating social media content, recording podcasts, and traveling the world, transforming lives.

Promise 4: I Will *Bless* Those Who *Bless* You

Moving to Denver required blessings from others.

My friend Aaron drove my U-Haul from Marshall to Denver. My mom made countless financial contributions to my vision. Various family members sowed into my dreams as well.

When God promised me this, I had no idea what it meant. I did not know that people would pay my rent and car notes and do kind acts to help me.

You know what they say— closed mouths don't get fed. For God to make good on this promise, I had to open my mouth and ask for help when needed, knowing that God would bless those who decided to bless me.

Promise 5: All The Families On Earth Will Be Blessed Through You

At this point, I knew I was in over my head. Naw, God, you chose the wrong person. There is nothing Cordarius, from Marshall, Texas, can do that will impact all the families on Earth. Even if I moved to Denver, how would all the families be blessed through me?

Again, I took it literally, but I now can see what God meant by this.

I am an author, podcaster, teacher, social media influencer, and pastor.

So yes, all the families I come in contact with will be blessed through me. My words will lead someone to a better life.

Faithful Obedience

God's five promises would only happen if I moved to Denver. I had a choice to make. I could either stay in Marshall, where things were comfortable, or move to Denver.

Obviously, I moved to Denver, and the rest is history.

God is still delivering on His promises because I have remained faithful and obedient to what He tells me to do. Moving to Denver was just the first yes that God needed me to say. Since then, my life has become a life of yeses. Saying yes is all I know how to do, even when I do not see what's on the other side.

To journey from hurting to healing, I encourage you to find a place where you can put yourself in a position to hear from

God. No social media, Netflix, or anything that can distract you.

Seek clarity on your next steps, and God will reveal them to you. What you do not understand now, you will understand later. Remember that healing is a process that doesn't happen at the snap of a finger.

Remain faithful and obedient, and watch God deliver on his promises.

Put The Work In

Reflect and answer these questions. Elaborate more in your journal if the provided space isn't enough.

1. How is your prayer life?

____

____

____

2. Have you ever fasted before? If so, when will you fast again? If not, then why?

____

____

____

3. When was the last time you heard God? What did he say to you?

____

____

____

4. What is God currently directing you to do?

    ____

    ____

    ____

5. In what ways do you hear God in your life?

    ____

    ____

    ____

6. Where is a place you can go to disconnect from everything?

    ____

    ____

    ____

7. On a scale of 1-10, with 1 being the lowest and 10 the highest, where would you rate your level of faith? Why?

    ____

    ____

    ____

8. What are practical steps you can implement in your life to increase your faith?

    a. ____

    b. ____

    c. ____

9. Survey your life and identify who, or what, is keeping you from having stronger faith. List them below.

    a. ____

    b. ____

    c. ____

10. It's one thing to have faith in God; it's another to have faith in his ability to do what he said. What is God speaking over your life?

____

____

____

CHAPTER 12

Therapy Will Save Your Life
Every Fruit Has A Root

Your Heart Deserves To Heal

Do you remember when you would fall and scrape your knee as a kid? How long did it take you to heal? How long did it take for the scab to grow and become itchy and irritating?

I remember the scabs taking at least a week to grow and three weeks to go away! It is hard to believe that a scraped knee from a fall took a month to heal! That's crazy, huh?

Life is the same way. One fall can take years to heal! You go through itchy and irritating seasons that seem to linger on forever! You suffer for a whole season for one mistake.

Metaphorically speaking, can you think of something that happened to you recently, or even as far back as your childhood, that caused you to bleed? Did you ever correctly heal from it, or did you push it so far back into your memory that you forgot about it?

Emotionally, we go through traumas that cause us to bleed profusely, with the only difference being that the heart can't heal like the skin can. Your skin can heal within a month, but your heart could take years.

The trauma(s) that you have been through have made you build protective walls around your heart without ever properly healing its wounds. You deserve to live with a healthy heart and not a damaged one!

Your heart deserves to heal.

Identify The Root

Just as there are benefits of living life with a healthy heart, there are unfortunate consequences of living life with a hurting one, such as narcissism, negativity, and toxicity.

There has to be a point in your life when you decide to stop living with a hurting heart. Eventually, you must realize that you need to identify the root of what has hurt you and address it to produce better fruit.

For every fruit, there's a root. When you decide to be rooted in healing, you will begin to produce fruit so pure that it will purify you and everyone you're connected to.

So, what do you do if you have noticed you are producing fruit from a hurting heart? Sever the root immediately. Disconnect from the source that is producing contaminated fruit. That source may be your family, friends, trauma, social media, or even a mindset that is not aligned with God's will for your healing.

When I was around the age of 10, I was introduced to my first pornographic film. Porn eventually led to masturbation, and masturbation eventually led to sex.

I was in this cycle for all of my teenage years. It wasn't until I was 28 that I understood my struggles with porn, masturbation, and premarital sex were rooted in the sexual abuse I experienced as a child.

One trauma can lead to a whole branch of impure fruit. My trauma caused me to be impure through my teenage years, and throughout my 20s, it blinded me from who I really was.

If you want to save years of your life, you need to identify the root of your problems.

It gets messy. It's not fun. You will want to quit; however, you cannot give up because, on the other side of severing your roots, is a life you can't even imagine.

Never in a million years did I imagine being an author, podcaster, or even traveling the world to share my story. I never thought I would heal and transform millions of lives, but here I am.

If you do not identify the root cause of your problems, your best years will never be seen on this side of life.

In the next chapter, I will discuss how I *identified* the root of my fruit, *communicated it, and embraced* who God created me to be.

Fighting Monsters In The Dark

My oldest son, Deuce, is going through the "fear of the dark" phase. He will not go into a dark room without me. He thinks monsters are lurking in the dark, waiting to fight him. If it were light in the room, he would fight the monsters alone, but when it is dark, he won't.

I realized that he isn't afraid of the monsters; he's just scared of the dark, so he doesn't fight monsters alone in the dark. He wants someone by his side to go into the dark with him to fight the monsters.

I go to therapy because I can not fight against monsters that lurk in the dark by myself. I need my therapist to fight with me. He has helped me turn on lights so my monsters aren't lurking in the dark.

I would have never been able to change my fruit if my therapist hadn't gone with me into a very dark place to help me fight my monsters and identify my roots.

It can be scary for you to travel into dark places to fight your monsters alone. You need a therapist to help you fight your demons and turn on your subconscious lights!

If you want to transform your life, you need to find a therapist. It is non-negotiable. Your life will change in ways you can't even imagine! You will start legacies and pass down blessings. Your grandkid's children will live a light-filled life because you decided to go to therapy.

The Truth About Therapy

My brain is the motor of my family. What good is my family if my brain is hurting? Staying in Denver taught me how to utilize therapy to save my brain.

One of the biggest game changers staying in Denver was the conversation around therapy. Everyone I knew had a therapist, and they encouraged me to find one. I also encourage you to find one.

I have a friend who was on the fence about therapy and thought that she didn't need one. She eventually took my advice and tried it, and now she can't go without it! She craves her weekly visits to her therapist! She told me she wished she would have started sooner, but her misconceptions kept her from going.

Growing up, we were taught that we do not need other people to help us with our problems. We were told that whatever happened in our house stayed in our house. Consequently, mindsets such as this have shut the door on therapy.

The media also adds a negative connotation to therapy. One thing I have noticed is that those who have never been to therapy are the ones with the strongest opinions about it. Shouldn't it be the other way around? Why not try it and then form an opinion?

Therapists are like doctors. When we are sick, we go to the doctor for advice on what to do next. Just as a doctor can advise us on the next steps in our lives, a therapist can too.

Therapists are miracle workers sent by God to heal your brain. Your brain can't heal if you don't reveal your darkest thoughts.

My therapist is the best friend my money pays for. I pay for his honesty and his loyalty. He, by law, will not tell anyone what I struggle with. I can be completely honest with him, and he can keep it real with me so that I can heal. I do not have to lie to him about how I am really doing.

Not being entirely forthcoming about your thoughts will water the root of your trauma, leading to more undesirable fruit. However, being honest with your therapist plants new seeds where new roots can grow, and desirable fruit can be produced.

My therapist is sent from God to help me fight my monsters that are in the dark. He guides me to enlightenment so that I can live a healed life.

When you make time for therapy, everything in your life will change. Your job situation will change. Your household will change. You will change! Find a therapist! Your life will change when you find a therapist.

Put The Work In

Here are three tips that will help you find a therapist.

1. **Check your insurance**. Most insurances cover therapy through the Employee Assistance Program (EAP). If they do, you'll get a list of insurance-covered therapists. This means that therapy will either be free or at a minimal co-pay. I have a friend who only pays $30 per visit, and she has a very high-quality therapist who is changing her life. Times have changed, and insurance covers therapy, so check it.

2. **Do a Google search**. Type in the search bar "therapists near me." Choose a website, and find a therapist that you think you like. Please do your research on the letters behind their name. Just like health doctors, therapists can specialize in different things. Research each acronym and what they mean. Do your homework before you select your new best friend. Make sure what you are healing from and who you choose to walk you through this are compatible. For instance, my therapist is a Certified Clinical Trauma Professional (CCTP). He specializes in identifying trauma and helping people move past it.

3. **Ask your friend who their therapist is**. If that person is good for them, that person will also be good for you. Can we normalize regular conversations about therapy in our

relationships and amongst our friend groups? If you are the only one in your friend group with a therapist, you may be called to help them heal. In the next chapter, I will discuss how essential it is to have people in your circle with whom you can be vulnerable and transparent.

—— **CHAPTER 13** ——

Exploring Transparency & Vulnerability
Part 1: Nakedness With Your Spouse

Transparency is the ability to be honest when you are asked a question. For example, what would be your initial response if your spouse asked you how you were doing, no matter how you felt? The answer to this question will determine how transparent you are.

Your first reflex may be to hide behind mantras such as, "I don't want to dump my issues on him," or "As the man, I have to be strong, and I can't display emotions." Both replies are crutches to transparency and drastically hinder the transformation from hurting to healing.

Vulnerability is the ability to share the truth without being asked. To be a vulnerable person goes entirely against the status quo. Vulnerability is opening doors that aren't knocked on. Confessing what you struggle with is an example of vulnerability. Do you have the ability to come forward with information that you could actually take to your grave? If not, then focusing on becoming more vulnerable is your next play. I get it; it's a struggle to discuss what's in your head without being asked, but I also know that doing so will accelerate your transformation.

Having someone to be transparent and vulnerable with is critical as you transform your life. Everyone needs someone. We are not created to be alone.

My Person: Bone From Bone, Flesh From Flesh

One of the biggest hindrances to healing is the lack of nakedness with your spouse. If you are married, your spouse should be your best friend. This is hard because we are intrinsically and culturally wired not to share our emotions. We are taught that crying is a weakness and that we should keep our heads down, suck it up, and work through it. This is the furthest thing away from the truth, creating separation in a marriage.

We need to fight the status quo and let our spouses be our best friends. You do not have to bear it all by yourself! Opening up to your spouse will open up doors in your relationship and transform you as a person!

In Genesis 2, Eve was created from Adam's rib. When he saw his bride, he was overcome with emotion and said, "This one is bone from my bone. And flesh from my flesh."

There are 206 bones in the human body. From head to toe, our bones are connected, providing structure and support for our whole body! In fact, when you break a bone, the entire body is affected.

Bones are strong, but still need flesh to help hold everything together. Bones and flesh work together to keep the body together, growing, and healthy.

In the same way, husband and wife work together to keep their body strong and together. You were not created to keep your mental health battles to yourself. You deserve support, too.

The speed of your transformation hinges on your ability to be transparent and vulnerable with your spouse. This also means you must learn to listen without being judgmental. We must support each other, even if we do not completely understand the struggle.

Living with someone who you can't be transparent and vulnerable with is counterintuitive, and it puts a cap on how far you go in your journey from hurting to healing.

You can not transform if you do not view your spouse as bone from your bone and flesh from your flesh. Your condition, physically, mentally, spiritually, and emotionally, directly affects your spouse since y'all are one body.

Whatever you are going through on the inside can be felt and seen on the outside unless you've mastered the art of masking it. Even then, spouses can still sense when something isn't right.

Discussing what is happening inside your head can be nerve-wracking and frightening. Still, the benefits of speaking up far outweigh the consequences of not saying anything at all.

Naked With No Shame

After Adam and Eve were created, we can read how they walked in the Garden of Eden, naked with no shame– what a life!

Being emotionally naked with your spouse is the fastest way to heal. Emotional nakedness is being an open book about your emotions. Identifying and communicating emotions is hard, but doing so creates a deeper level of intimacy between you and your spouse.

Too often, we run to sex to bury what we are feeling on the inside. Sex is not the answer to your problems. It only provides a temporary reprieve from the emotions that you are feeling. However, being transparent and vulnerable opens the door for your partner to actively participate in your healing.

Not only does emotional nakedness heal you, but it also creates another level of intimacy that enhances sex. When you are honest with your spouse about your most hurtful experiences, it creates a sense of security that allows you to enjoy other areas of your marriage more.

In Denver, some trials and tests opened the door for emotional nakedness between Shundra and me. We began to have conversations more frequently about my feelings and what was going on in my head. I slowly began to share more with her about my mental health, which was very hard for me.

I can remember a conversation that I had with her at our bathroom sink, where, for the first time, I poured my heart out to her. When I was through, she asked me two questions. I didn't like them, but they changed my life.

She asked, "Are you happy to be alive?" and "Do you need medicine?"

Initially, I was heated. I felt she did not understand what I was trying to tell her, but that was not true. It took me a couple of days to digest what she asked before I finally understood the message.

She would never tell me anything that would jeopardize my well-being because she understands that the trajectory of our family hinges on my brain's health.

Shundra is literally me outside of me, listening and talking to me. She feels me. She sees me. She understands me. So when I hurt, she hurts. When I heal, she heals.

Unlocking Your Spouse's Purpose

Being emotionally naked with Shundra brought out her created purpose. When I was broken, she supported me. When my flesh was tired, she held everything together.

By being emotionally naked with Shundra, I opened up the door to her purpose, which is to be my helper. When I am empty, she fills me up. When I feel weak, she strengthens me. When I am only a shell of myself, she holds me up. She is my person, created just right for me. She is the inside of me, in human form.

If I am being frank with you, I still have thoughts of insignificance, and every time I do, I tell Shundra, and she supports me and holds me up every single time. Our spouses can not help us if they do not know what is happening.

Emotional nakedness with your spouse is a pivotal step to unlocking healing in your life.

In marriage, it is critical to understand that our spouses are directly affected when we hurt. This is why a lack of transparency and vulnerability is detrimental to the health of the marriage. Your spouse has the right to know everything that goes on in your head that could affect her. Keeping secrets will not heal you.

Being transparent and vulnerable with your spouse means learning to be quiet and take their advice. Hearing your spouse tell you about you can be challenging and often uncomfortable. Knowing how to release your emotions, receive feedback, and reflect on what was said is very important.

When you are at your sink, pouring out your tears to your spouse, always remember that God sent them personally to heal you, so let them. Learn how to be naked with no shame— it will shift you and your marriage from hurting to healing.

Put The Work In

1. Why do you think being transparent and vulnerable with your spouse is hard?

____

____

____

2. Secrets can turn a relationship upside down. Please pray for an opportunity to have a serious talk with your spouse. Below, brainstorm a what, when, where, and how approach to transparency with your spouse.

   a. What do you need to be emotionally naked about?

   ____

   ____

   ____

   b. When is a good time for you to do it?

   ____

   ____

   ____

c. Where is a good place for you to have an honest
    conversation?

    86

    ____

    ____

    ____

d. How do you plan to approach the conversation?

    ____

    ____

    ____

CHAPTER 14

Exploring Transparency & Vulnerability
PART 2: Nakedness With Your Friends

Your Circle Of Influence

Who can you be transparent with if you do not have a spouse? The answer is your circle of influence. It is important to have at least one person you can share your heart with.

A circle of influence is a group of friends, typically less than five people– most are lucky to have three. This group of friends laughs with you, cries with you, and takes your secrets to the grave for you. They give you practical life advice. They offer insight into your life that makes you see yourself for who God created you to be.

If you and your friends aren't open and honest with each other, then y'all aren't friends; y'all are associates. True friendship is more than just lounges, clubs, and fun times. It is also the dark, challenging times you do not know how to overcome.

How long you have known a person isn't the only indicator of a good friend, and just because y'all grew up together doesn't mean that they have your best interest at heart.

Transparency and vulnerability are underrated and overlooked qualities in a friend. The true measure of a best friend is not only their ability to hear you but also their ability to share their struggles with you. You should be in a mutually beneficial friendship, not a one-sided one. You should be able to talk to them, and they should be able to talk to you. Be cautious of friendships where you are the only one sharing rainy days.

Solitary Confinement

The prison system's worst form of punishment is solitary confinement. When the prisoner constantly breaks the rules or poses a hazard to others, the guards move him away from the general population and place him in a small room the size of a mall parking space. The prisoner then goes 23 hours a day with no human interaction. They eat, sleep, and defecate in the same space. This punishment is cruel and unusual, meant to teach the prisoner a lesson.

Sadly, many choose to live their life in solitary confinement because they have been betrayed one too many times. They believe isolation is safer because the deepest wounds came from those they trusted most.

Just because you have been burned and betrayed doesn't mean that you should place yourself in solitary confinement. Maybe you should choose your circle a little bit more wisely. It is not healthy to be alone. Everyone needs a team.

Solomon says in Ecclesiastes 4:7-8, "I observed yet another example of something *meaningless* under the sun. This is the case of a man who is all *alone*, without a child or a brother, yet who works hard to gain as much wealth as he can. But then he asks himself, 'Who am I working for? Why am I giving up so much pleasure now?' It is all so *meaningless* and *depressing*."

The wisest man in the Bible says that it doesn't matter how hard you work to become wealthy; if you isolate yourself and have no one to share it with, it is all meaningless and depressing. Solomon is saying that everyone deserves companionship, and if you do not have it, then you risk being sad and depressed all your life.

Better Together

I used to work for a company with a cultural tenet centered around being better together. They had a philosophy that isolationism was not in their employees' best interests. They made it their priority to create systems that fostered workplace companionship. Solomon agrees with this principle because he said two people are better off than one, for they can help each other succeed.

If companionship is practiced in the workplace and proven in the Bible, why do we not apply it to our personal lives?

You are not better alone. You can not live life by yourself. You need companionship. A good friend helps you when you have fallen into depression. A good friend grabs your hand when you've fallen down.

It is hard to heal from life's traumas if you have committed yourself to living alone. You need to give at least one person the key to your heart so that they can help you when you're hurting.

It is important to note that just because you have a close friend doesn't mean you will not be attacked. However, having a friend who will stand back-to-back with you while you handle life's problems is a cheat code that'll help you transform from hurting to healing.

Put The Work In

In the circle below, write down everyone in your circle of influence and your relationship to them. Reflect on how they have helped you in your most challenging times.

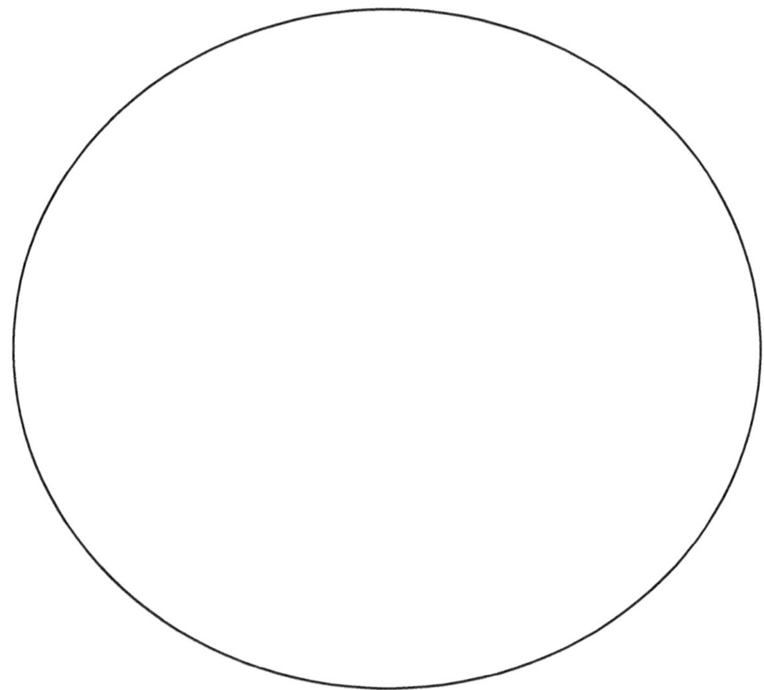

——— **CHAPTER 15** ———

Connected

People, Pain, Passion, and Purpose

The reason why it is hard for you to shift from hurting to healing is that you allow people who do not add value to your life to remain in it.

Sometimes, the value that people add to you is seasonal. They were only meant to be a part of your life for a period of time. You will not be able to move forward with seasonal friends in your circle. Do not be afraid to reassign those who don't bring value to your life.

When you survey your friends, ask yourself, "Are they producing fruit?" If the answer is no, and they are not salvageable, you must cut them off.

Think about a strawberry in a container that goes bad. What naturally happens to the rest of the strawberries in the container? Right, they go bad as well. This is called contamination. When one fruit is contaminated, the rest of the fruit connected to it is also contaminated. Beware of friends who are contaminated and connected to you! Their contamination will spill over into your life, leaving you to live without direction, vision, or purpose.

Connected To Your Purpose

It is important to have people around you who understand your pain, fuel your passion, and support your purpose.

Most importantly, you need to be connected to your purpose! Who you are connected to can disconnect you from your purpose, causing you to live a purposeless life.

You may be reading this, and you may not know your purpose. Can I let you in on a secret? Your purpose is hidden in your passion, and your passion can be found in your pain. Let me explain.

Growing up, I was raised by a single mom with three kids. I constantly wanted a relationship with a dad, an uncle, or a brother. I wanted a role model to teach me to play baseball and cheer me on from the stands. Someone who saw my purpose and cultivated it through intentional mentorship.

My mom got married when I was about 12 years old, but that didn't erase the pain of not having anyone there before then. The traumas that I dealt with before the age of 12 could have been alleviated if I had a strong dad, uncle, or brother consistently in my life.

The pain of not having a father turned into my purpose, which is to coach you from hurting to healing so that you can maximize your life.

Do you see what I did there? I took my pain, turned it into purpose, and built a business that allows me to be the person I needed when I was a kid.

Purposeful Connections

Knowing your purpose controls who you are connected to.

I cannot say enough about how important it is to have people around you who have pain, passion, and purpose. If you have friends around you who do not have a purpose in life, you will be contaminated with that same mindset, no matter how healthy and strong you think you are.

I remember when I was in my younger 20s, I was connected to friends who didn't know their purpose, and because I was connected to them, I was disconnected from my purpose.

Who you choose to be connected to matters. Survey the people around you. Are you connected to people who are disconnected from their purpose?

In 1 Samuel 20, Jonathan and David had a very strong friendship. Their connection was so strong that when Jonathan's dad, King Saul, wanted to kill David, Jonathan still decided to stay friends with David. Jonathan's love for David was so strong that he loved David as himself.

A friend like Jonathan will encourage you when you have no joy. He will cry with you when you are sad. He knows your greatest sorrow and will not tell a soul. He helps you heal when you are hurting. He stands on business and will always fight with you.

Put The Work In

95

1. In 1-2 sentences, answer the following questions:

    a. What has brought you pain?

    ____

    ____

    ____

    b. What are you passionate about?

    ____

    ____

    ____

    c. What is your purpose?

    ____

    ____

    ____

CHAPTER 16

The Truth About Healing

If you've made it this far in the book, then there's no doubt that your mind has started to view things differently. Maybe you've been applying ICE to your life, being STILL, or have decided to go to therapy. Regardless of what you have taken away from this book, there's more that I need to tell you.

In this chapter, I will give you a few truths about healing. It would be irresponsible of me to motivate you to heal and not tell you the truth about healing.

As we conclude our time together in this book, I want you to stay locked in and internalize what I am about to tell you.

Healing is Hard, and it Hurts

If healing were easy, everyone would do it.

It's hard bouncing back from a broken heart. It's hard to overcome sexual abuse. It's hard to look at a parent who abandoned you as a child. It's hard to look at the person who hurt you as they frolic around the Earth like they haven't done anything. It hurts to heal when what you are healing from has your emotions off balance.

It hurts when you walk into rooms where you're the only one healing. It's hard to have conversations with people whose hurt oozes from their mouths, but they do not see it or care to heal if you point it out. It's even harder to talk to someone who is transparent and vulnerable about what they are going through, but will not go to therapy if you advise them to do so.

Your skin will crawl. You will get irritated, but remember, healing is a journey one must accept. You can not force someone to heal. You have to keep healing and living your life.

The sad truth is that most people would rather hurt than heal because hurting is familiar and comfortable, and it's all that they know. It hurts to talk to people who are stuck in their ways.

Healing is hard and hurts because you will want people to take the journey with you, but that will not happen.

The sad reality is that the people closest to you will see your transformation and refuse to change themselves, even when they know they need to.

Do not let those you love discourage you. Their life is theirs, and only Jesus can save them, not you.

Healing Is Lonely

As I mentioned above, this is a personal journey that you have decided to take. You can not make anyone take this journey with you.

The truth is, many people do not want to face their traumas and hurts because they are so heavy. They fail to realize that if they take this journey, their life will elevate because the foundation is no longer their trauma; it'll be their healing.

It's lonely out here in these healing streets, fam. It ain't popular, it ain't sexy, and it doesn't feel good.

I go to therapy once a month, and the three weeks between sessions feel like watching grass grow. Your brain will wonder, you'll think things that you'll never tell anyone, and you will want to stop.

Do not stop! Find someone in your circle of influence to talk to in between therapy sessions. It's important.

Healing from trauma increases your emotional intelligence, so as you become more intelligent and more aware of emotions, others around you will not understand what you say because they are emotionally ignorant.

It's hard. It hurts. It's lonely.

But if it were easy, everyone would do it.

Healing Takes Time

I remember when I started my healing journey in January of 2023. I had started therapy, and I just knew that my journey would be fast. I was ready to tell the world that I had been healed! As I look back on it, it's funny because I was gravely mistaken.

The truth is that healing takes time. No matter how much you've healed, you can't outpace life. Life has a funny way of throwing things at you that will slow down your process.

For example, I started to heal in January of 2023. In February of that year, Shundra and I had our second son. In April, Shundra had three procedures done that required her to undergo anesthesia. Naturally, I had to pause my journey to care for my family.

Also, in April, God told me to quit my job. So, from April 15th to August 30th, my family was short about 5,000 dollars a month. I'll dive into this story in my next book, though.

The point is that life never stops life-ing, and there's no time frame on how long it'll take you to heal. You just have to go with the flow and handle what life throws your way.

If I didn't learn anything else, I learned this— whatever life throws your way while you are healing is meant to assist you on your journey, not hold you back.

Healing takes time, and you must be in it for the long haul.

Healing Is Rewarding

If you endure the course, healing is rewarding. The process isn't sexy and sometimes doesn't feel good. What I know from experience is that if you endure the course, your life will elevate exponentially.

Imagine running a race with a 45 lb weight attached to your ankle. Yeah, you wouldn't go very far. Living life with trauma is the same exact way. You can't run the race of life with dead weight attached to you.

In fact, the quality of your life is determined by the decision to keep running with the weight or to pause and detach so that you can run further, faster. When you heal from the thing that has been holding you back, your life will go so much further!

The truth is that many athletes train with weights attached because, when they remove them, their bodies become stronger and faster.

The same is true for your trauma. You have lived your whole life running with the weight of your trauma, but this is not a bad thing. Your traumas have made you stronger. They have made you faster. They have given you a story to tell.

Your trauma was a weight that wasn't meant to hold you back but instead was created to make you stronger, faster, more disciplined, and an overcomer.

The truth is that I won't be on Earth for eternity, but because I decided to journey from hurting to healing, generations that I will not be able to see will be able to read my writings, see my content, and walk in the freedom that I trailblazed for them.

My reward is the legacy I can create because I have decided to heal.

Just as we honor and idolize Martin Luther King, Rosa Parks, and Barack Obama for their contributions to the black community, my family will honor me for breaking generational curses. I made financial freedom possible. My decision to heal made internal peace possible for my seeds coming after me.

My reward is actually my why. I want my great-grandchildren to read this and know that their great-grandfather fought a good fight, finished his race, and kept the faith throughout.

As my family will honor me, yours will honor you, too. It won't be easy; it'll get lonely for a season and take some time, but the reward is worth it!

www.ingramcontent.com/pod-product-compliance
Lightning Source LLC
Chambersburg PA
CBHW071448130726
47997CB00006B/2280